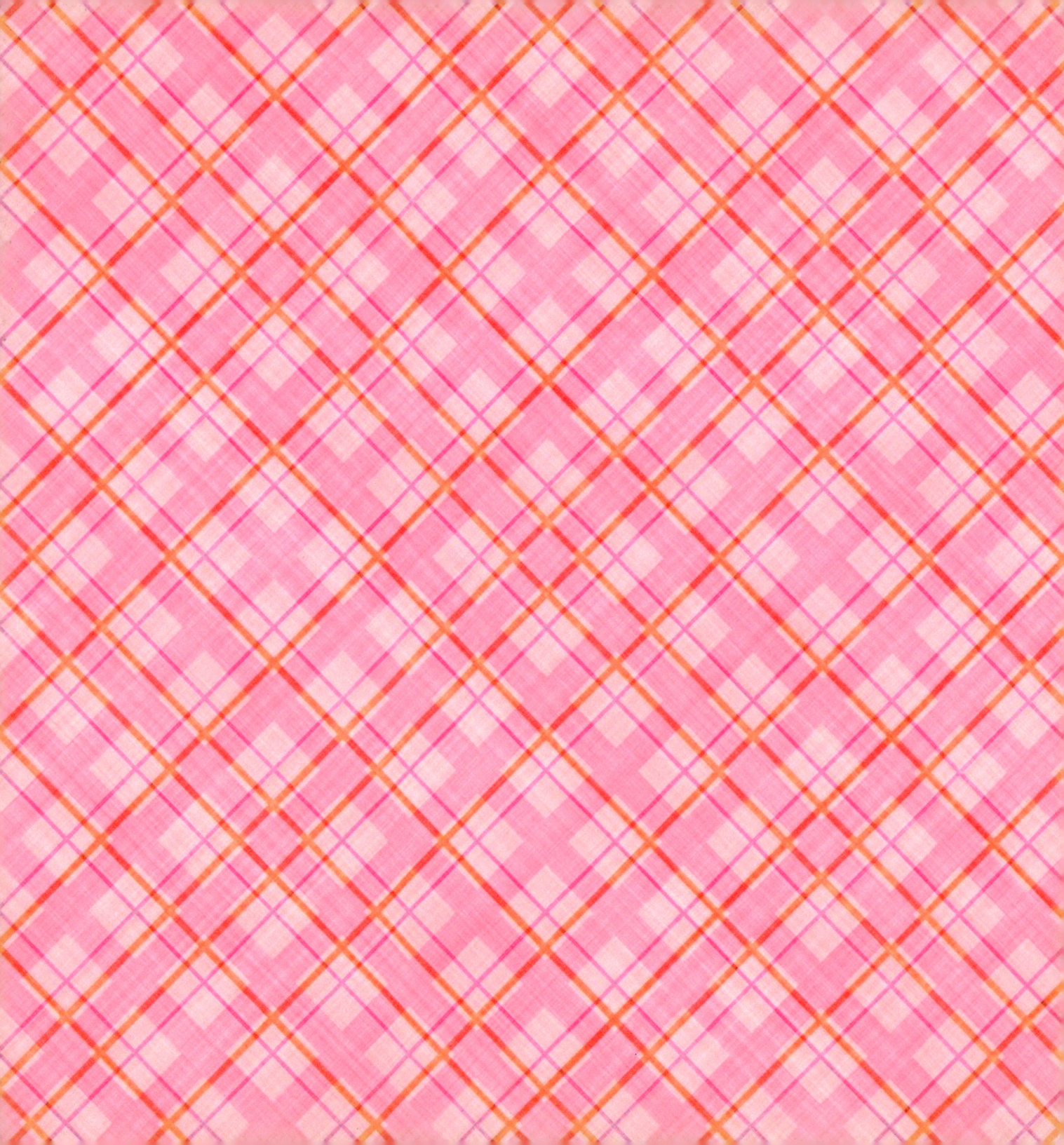

God Made Flowers

God made flowers: pansies, daisies, roses, buttercups

In the beginning, God created the heavens and the earth.

-Genesis 1:1

Beautifully arranged

Everywhere they grow

Playful fun

Psalms 112:1-2

Praise the LORD!

Holiday cheer

Garden accessories

Flowers are a gift every season, every year

Jeremiah 32:39
I will give them one heart and one way

Adorning a pasture

Birthday blessings

The fruit of the spirit is love.
-Galatians 5:22-23

A crown for my hair

Flowers are one of God's sweet creations

Perfume fills the air

Easter gifts

A springtime gesture

Accompanying a "Happily Ever After"

Isaiah 61:8-9

...I will make an everlasting covenant with them.

No matter the occasion, God made flowers a bouquet of love and cheer.

It is wonderful living in God's unity.
– Psalm 133:1

Flowers

What are your favorite flowers?

Have you ever made a wreath out of flowers or a bouquet?

Can you draw a picture of a flower garden?

How many flowers are in a dozen roses?

Our Father

Our Father, Who art in Heaven, hallowed be Thy name; Thy Kingdom come, Thy will be done on earth as it is in Heaven. Give us this day our daily bread; and forgive us our trespasses as we forgive those who trespass against us; and lead us not into temptation, but deliver us from evil. Amen.

Glory Be

Glory be to the Father and to the Son and to the Holy Spirit. As it was in the beginning is now, and ever shall be, world without end. Amen.

Copyright © 2017 by Elizabeth Terry

Copyright © 2017 Hand-painted Watercolor Artist Credit Inside

All rights reserved. No part of this publication may be reproduced in part, in whole or otherwise, electronically or in print, without permission from the publisher.

Gods Little Garden Books.com

This book is dedicated to Teresa – you are so sweet! These flowers are for you!

Copyright 2017 © FOTOLIA.com – FOTOLIA-Ghen, Any-li, Tanom, Andrea Danti, arxichtu4ki, cat_arch_angel, ovaleeva, pysfer, dariavstiagova, adelveys, a_kaz, Amy_Li, derbisheva, shibanuk, analginiz, luchioly, Kateryna, Tatyana, Yulia, Tanyacya, Anastezia, natali_mya, gribanessa, undrey, juliafast1977, maltiase, olga, arsvik, mitrushova, cmwatercolors, yanushkov, adelveys, olesyaturchuk, nutart, viktoriya Manvilova, ovaleeva, Marina, Knopazyzy, Silmairel, budogosh, mstislava, mesori, zzorik, lenavetka87, Homunkulus28, wacmoka, meduzzza, gribanessa, antinspring, Nadezda Kostina, aleksandrasmirnova, elenanmedmededeva, JaneLane, Olesyaturchuk, Koroleva8, nastyasklyarova, adelveys, anastasianio, nataliahubbert, yorikoKatayama, 4uda4ka, depiano, Koroleva8, Kostanproff, guykantawan, zenina, val_iva Lev, Insoles, InnaOgandoelennadzen, lisagerrard00, Yunako, Psartostudio, analgin12, izumikobayaski, dariaustiugova, agaes8080, Anna Ismagilova, PYRAMIS, idinka, German Ariel Beria

Copyright 2017 © SHUTTERSTOCK.COM SHUTTERSTOCK- Diana Taliun, Dora Zett, Africa Studio, MestoSveta, Cheryl E. Davis, sutsaiy, stockcreations, Milleflore Images, Vladimir Tronin, studiovin, allstars, Skrynnik Mariia, Natalka Dmitrova, Lena Vetka, Iya Balushkina, Nadezhda Shoshina, Analgin, Ruth Black, nadejdasweet, Windnight, Maria Komar, JL-Pfeifer, JasminkaM, Shyvoronkova Kateryna, Christopher Elwell, Wiktory, muh23 , Alison Henley, Pavel Korotkov, Myimagine, Agnes Kantaruk, Roboryba, Ecaterina Petrova, annadolzhenko, Faenkova Elena, Le Panda, Yunaco, ms. Octopus, art_of_sun, petrmalinak, Spa Chan, Olga Po, Karen Kaspar, BlueOrange Studio, Anastasiia Skliarova, ER_09, JP Chretien, vectorfusionart, DNKMN, arxichtu4ki, vnlit, MNStudio, TravnikovStudio, Kzenon, Vadim Ivanov, Ragnarock, Andrii Muzyka, Karen Sarraga, Aleksey Korchemkin, qwasder1987, Dora Zett, fotogestoeber, sarsmis, Elina Yevgrashkina, motorolka, KMNPhoto, Elena Shashkina, Barbara Neveu, Elena Medvedeva, Yasonya, Liudmila Fadzeyeva, Svetlana Prikhnenko, Kisialiou Yury, Grigorita Ko, Kuzina, Jula_Lily, Kotkoa, Epitavi, Warren Price Photography

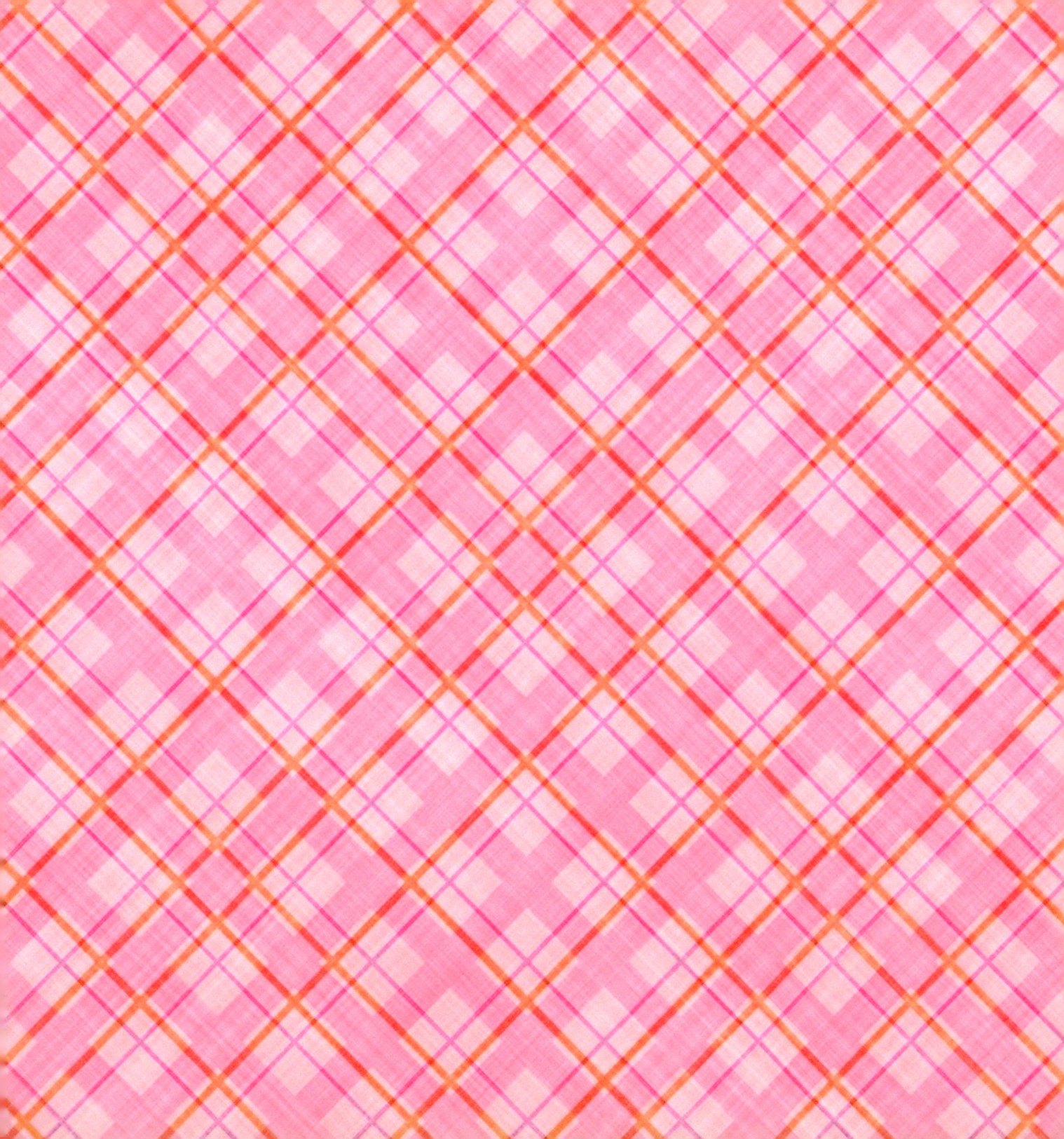

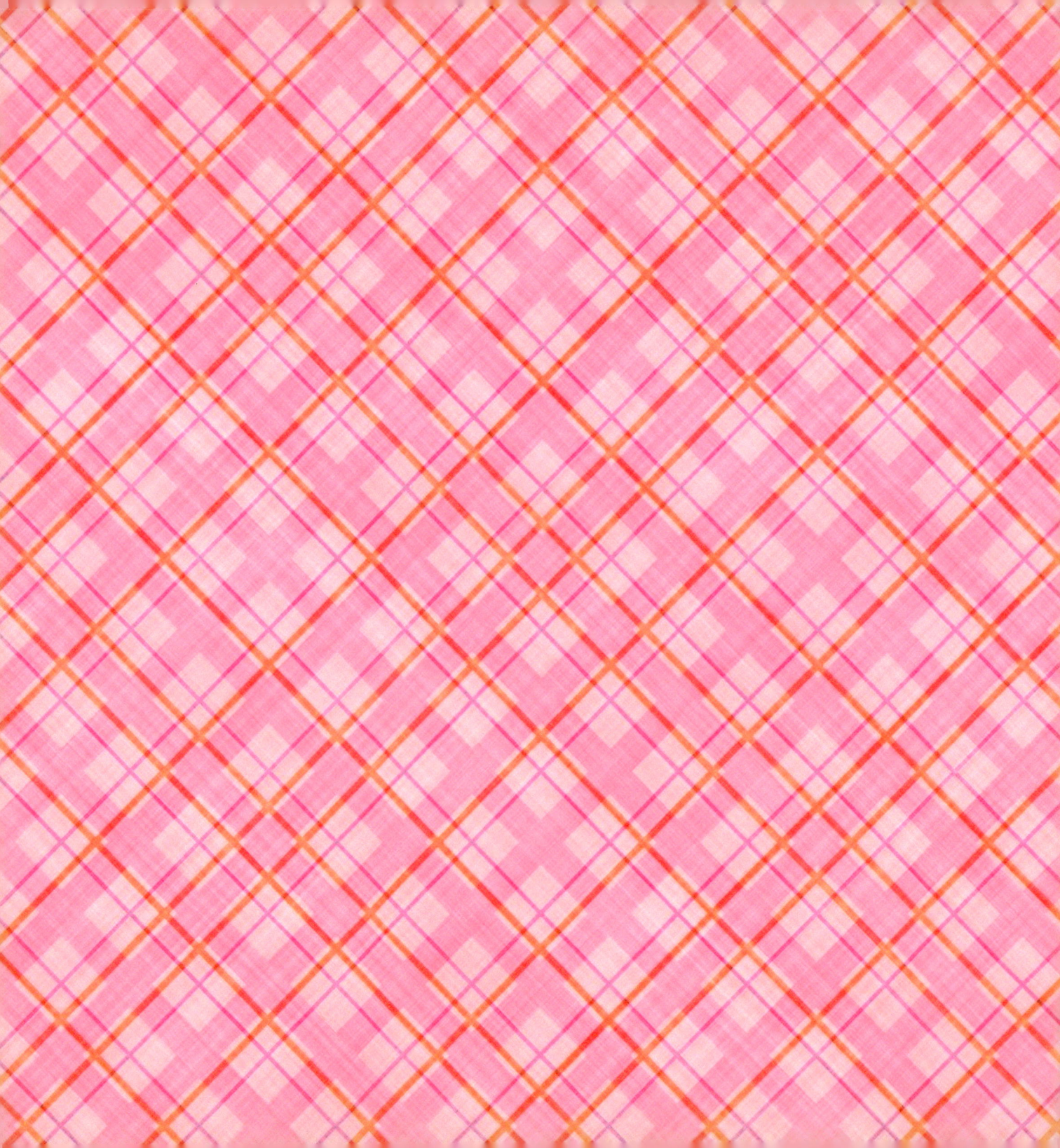

Made in United States
Cleveland, OH
22 December 2024